1	HSK1

爱

2	

八

3	HSK1

爸爸

4	HSK1

北京

1 HSK1 # ài to love, affection, to be fond of, to like	2 HSK1 # bā eight, 8
3 HSK1 # bà ba (informal) father, CL:個|个,位	4 HSK1 # Běi jīng Beijing, capital of People's Republic of China, Peking, PRC government

杯子

本

不

不客气

bēi zi

cup, glass,
CL:個|个,支,枝

běn

basis

bù

(negative prefix), not, no

bú kè qi

you're welcome, impolite,
rude, blunt, don't
mention it

菜

茶

吃

出租车

cài

dish (type of food), vegetables, vegetable, cuisine, CL:盤|盘,道

chá

tea, tea plant, CL:杯,壶|壶

chī

to eat, to have one's meal, to eradicate

chū zū chē

taxi

大

打电话

的

点

dà

Big

dǎ diàn huà

to make a telephone call

de

of, structural particle:
used before a noun

diǎn

point

电脑

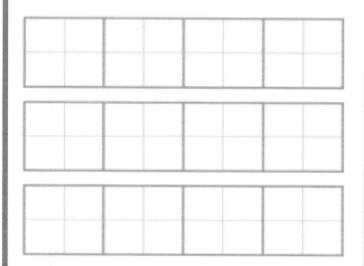

电视

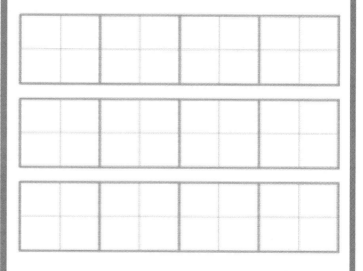

电影

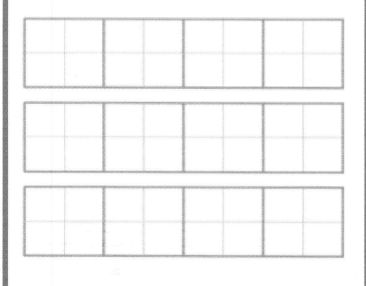

东西

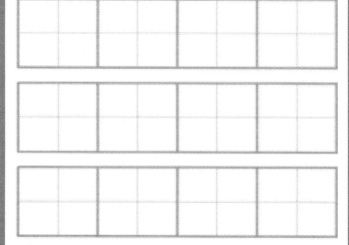

diàn nǎo

computer, CL:臺|台

diàn shì

television, TV,
CL:臺|台,個|个

diàn yǐng

movie, film,
CL:部,片,幕,場|场

dōng xi

thing, stuff, person,
CL:個|个,件

都

读

对不起

多

dōu

all, both, entirely (due to) each, even, already

dú

to read, to study, reading of word (i.e. pronunciation)

duì bu qǐ

I am sorry

duō

many, much, a lot of, numerous, multi-

多少

二

儿子

饭馆

duō shǎo

number, amount, somewhat

èr

two, 2, stupid (Beijing dialect)

ér zi

son

fàn guǎn

restaurant, CL:家

飞机

分钟

高兴

个

fēi jī

airplane, CL: 架

fēn zhōng

minute

gāo xìng

happy, glad, willing (to do sth), in a cheerful mood

gè

individual, this, that, size, classifier for people or objects in general

工作

狗

汉语

好

gōng zuò

jobs

gǒu

dog, CL:隻|只,條|条

Hàn yǔ

Chinese language, CL:門|门

hǎo

good, well, proper, good to, easy to

和

喝

很

回

37 HSK1	38 HSK1
hé and, together with, with, sum, union, peace	**hē** to drink, to shout (a command), My goodness!
39 HSK1	40 HSK1
hěn (adverb of degree), quite, very, awfully	**huí** return

会

火车站

家

叫

huì

can, be possible, be able to, will, be likely to

huǒ chē zhàn

train station

jiā

Family

jiào

to shout, to call, to order, to ask

今天

九

开

看见

jīn tiān

today, at the present, now

jiǔ

nine, 9

kāi

open

kàn jiàn

to see, to catch sight of

块

来

老师

了

kuài

Piece

lái

to come, to arrive, to come round, ever since, next

lǎo shī

teacher, CL:個|个,位

le

(modal particle intensifying preceding clause), (completed action marker)

冷

里

零

六

lěng

cold

lǐ

lining, interior, inside, internal, also written 裡|里

líng

zero

liù

six, 6

吗

妈妈

买

猫

ma

(question tag)

mā ma

mom

mǎi

to buy, to purchase

māo

cat, CL:隻|只

没

没关系

米饭

明天

méi

(negative prefix for verbs), have not, not

méi guān xi

it doesn't matter

mǐ fàn

(cooked) rice

míng tiān

tomorrow

名字

那

哪

那儿

míng zi

name (of a person or thing), CL:個|个

nà

that, those, then (in that case)

nǎ

how, which

nà r

there

哪儿

呢

能

你

nǎ r

where?, wherever, anywhere

ne

(question particle for subjects already mentioned)

néng

to be able to, to be capable of, ability, capability

nǐ

you (informal, as opposed to polite 您)

nián

year, CL:個|个

nǚ ér

daughter

péng you

friend, CL:個|个,位

piào liang

pretty, beautiful

苹果

七

钱

前面

píng guǒ

apple, CL:個|个,顆|颗

qī

seven, 7

qián

coin, money, CL:筆|笔

qián miàn

ahead, in front, preceding, above

请

去

热

人

qǐng

to ask, to invite, please (do sth), to treat (to a meal etc), to request

qù

to go

rè

heat, to heat up, fervent, hot (of weather), warm up

rén

man, person, people, CL:個|个,位

认识

日

三

商店

rèn shi

to know, to recognize, to be familiar with

rì

sun, day, date, day of the month, abbr. for 日本|日本 Japan

sān

three, 3

shāng diàn

store, shop, CL:家,個|个

上午

少

谁

什么

shàng wǔ

morning, CL:個|个

shǎo

few, little, lack

shéi

who, also pronounced shui2

shén me

what?, who?, something, anything

十

是

时候

书

shí

ten, 10

shì

is, are, am, yes, to be

shí hou

time, length of time, moment, period

shū

book, letter, CL:本,冊|册,部, see also 書經|书经 Book of History

水

睡觉

说话

四

shuǐ

water, river, liquid, beverage

shuì jiào

to go to bed, to go to sleep

shuō huà

to speak, to say, to talk, to gossip, to tell stories, talk, word

sì

four, 4

岁

她

他

太

suì

classifier for years (of age), year, year (of crop harvests)

tā

she

tā

he or him, (used for either sex when the sex is unknown or unimportant)

tài

too

天气

听

同学

喂

tiān qì

weather

tīng

to listen, to hear, to obey

tóng xué

(fellow) classmate, CL:位,個|个

wèi

hello (interj., esp. on telephone), hey, to feed (sb or some animal)

我

我们

五

喜欢

wǒ

I, me, my

wǒ men

we, us, ourselves, our

wǔ

five, 5

xǐ huan

to like, to be fond of

下

下午

下雨

先生

xià

down, downwards, below, lower, later

xià wǔ

afternoon, p.m., CL:個|个

xià yǔ

to rain, rainy

xiān sheng

teacher, Mister (Mr.), husband, doctor (topolect), CL:個|个,位

现在

想

小

小姐

xiàn zài

now, at present, at the moment, modern, current, nowadays

xiăng

to think, to believe, to suppose, to wish, to want, to miss

xiăo

small, tiny, few, young

xiăo jie

Miss

写

些

谢谢

星期

xiě

to write

xiē

some, few, several, (a measure word)

xiè xie

to thank, thanks

xīng qī

week, CL:個|个

学生

学习

学校

一

xué sheng

student, school child

xué xí

to learn, to study

xué xiào

school

yī

one, 1, single, a (article), as soon as

衣服

医生

医院

椅子

yī fu

clothes, CL:件,套

yī shēng

doctor

yī yuàn

hospital

yǐ zi

chair, CL:把,套

有

月

在

再见

yǒu

to have, there is, there are, to exist, to be

yuè

moon, month,
CL:個|个,輪|轮

zài

in

zài jiàn

goodbye, see you again later

怎么

怎么样

这

这儿

zěn me

how?, what?, why?

zěn me yàng

how?, how about?, how was it?, how are things?

zhè

this, these, (commonly pr. zhei4 before a classifier, esp. in Beijing)

zhè r

here

中国

中午

住

桌子

Zhōng guó

China, Middle Kingdom

zhōng wǔ

noon, midday, CL:個|个

zhù

to live, to dwell, to stay, to reside, to stop

zhuō zi

table, desk, CL:張|张,套

字

坐

做

昨天

zì

word

zuò

sit

zuò

to do, to make, to produce, to write

zuó tiān

yesterday

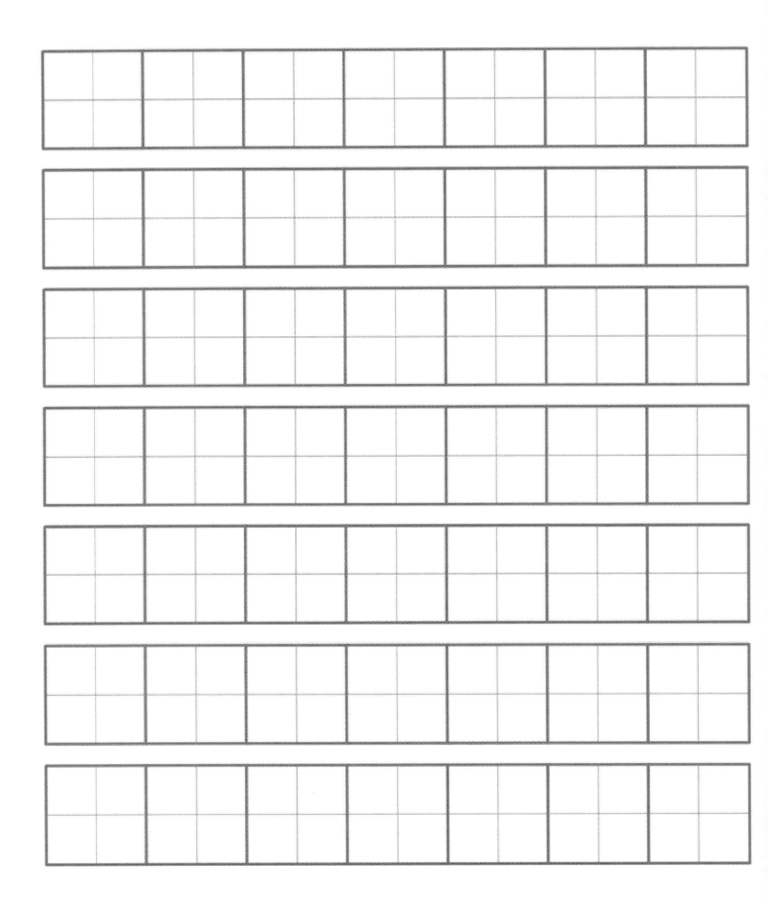

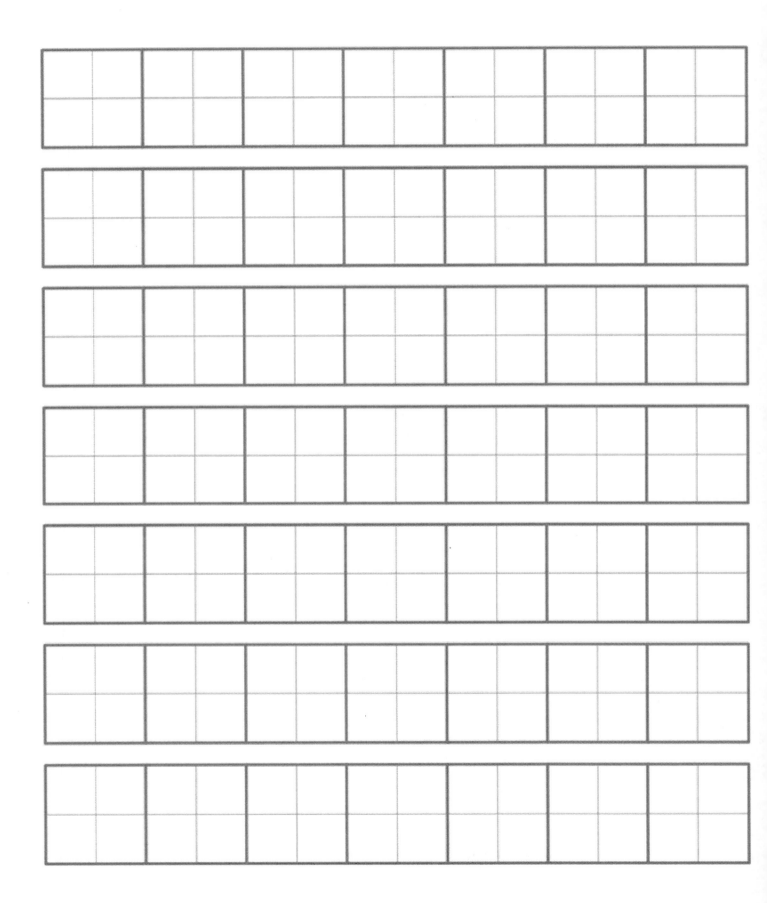

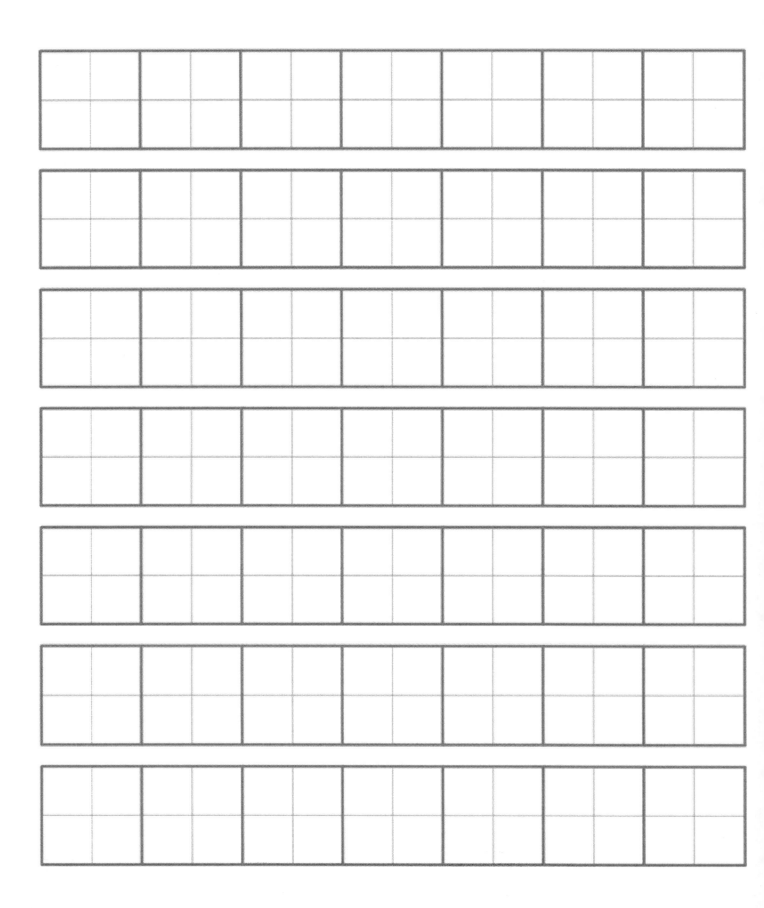

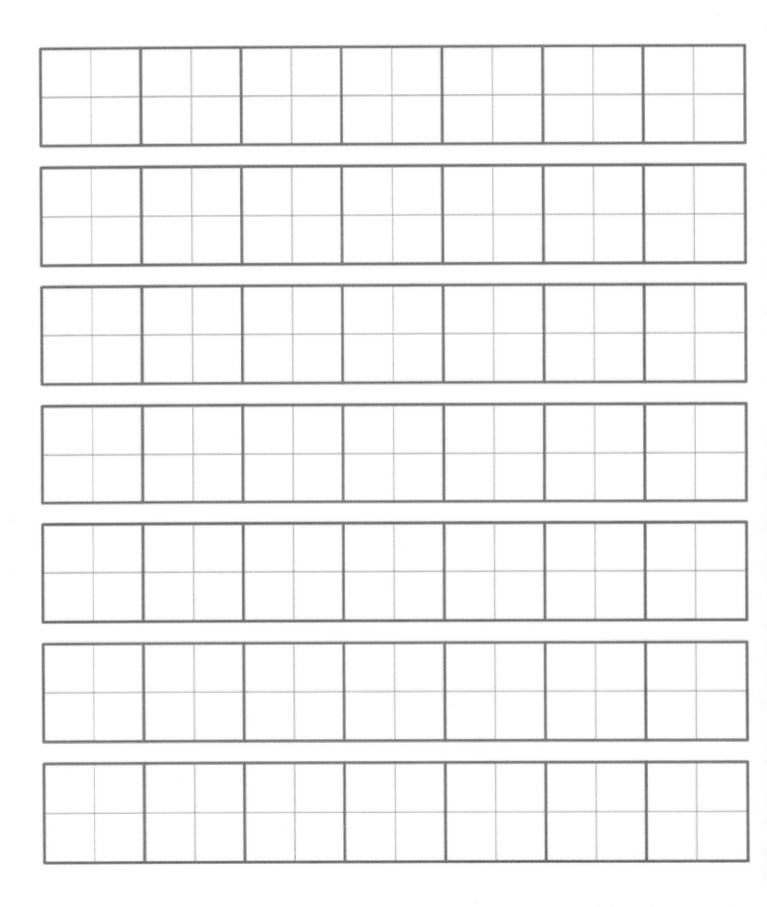

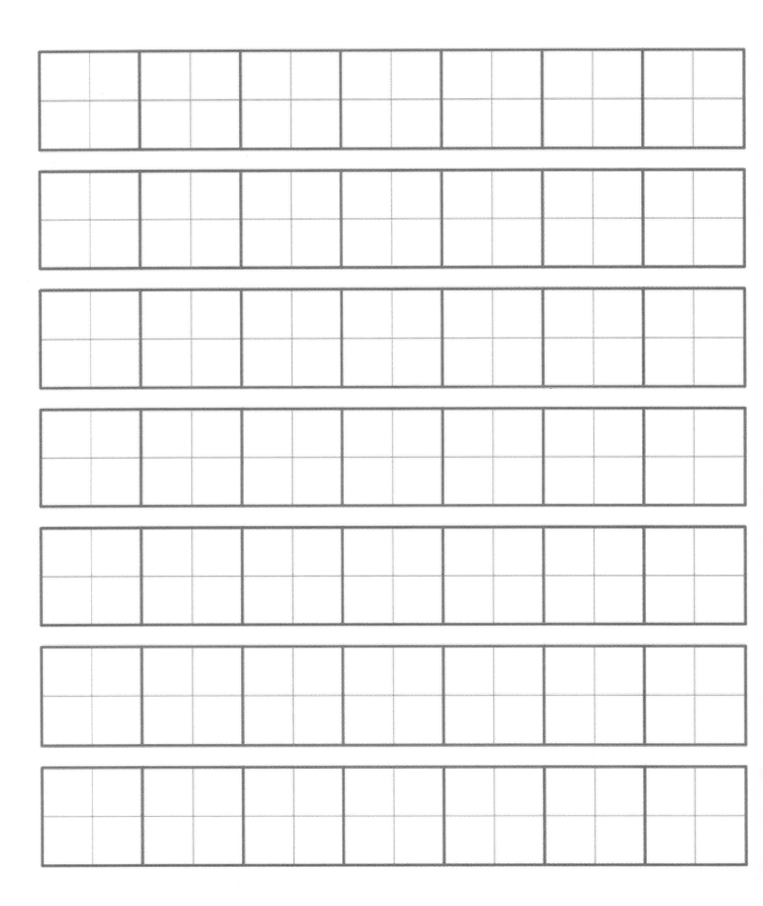

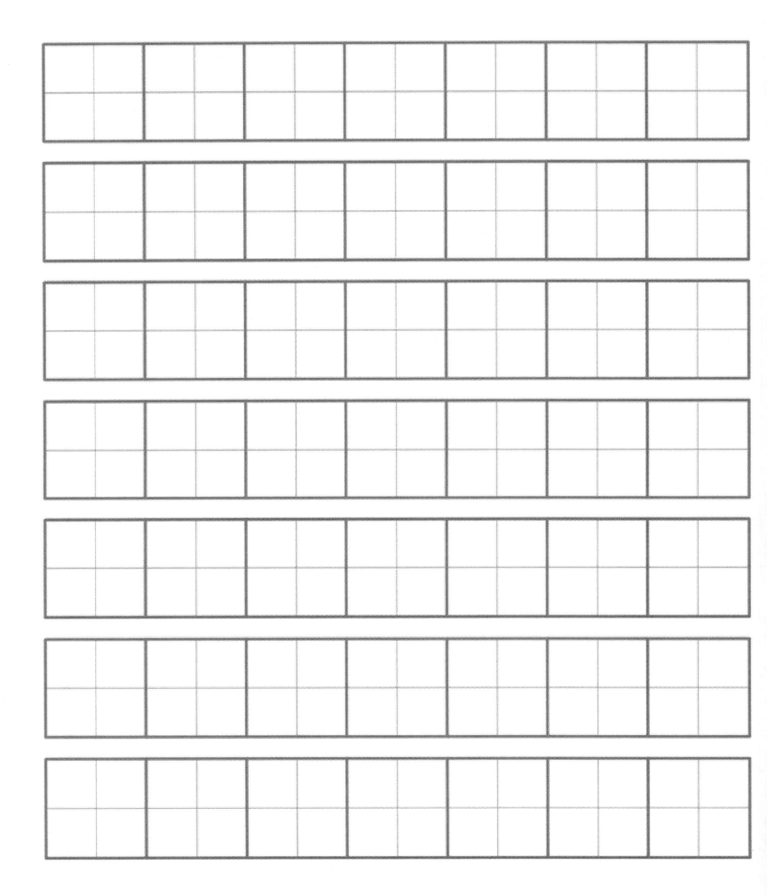

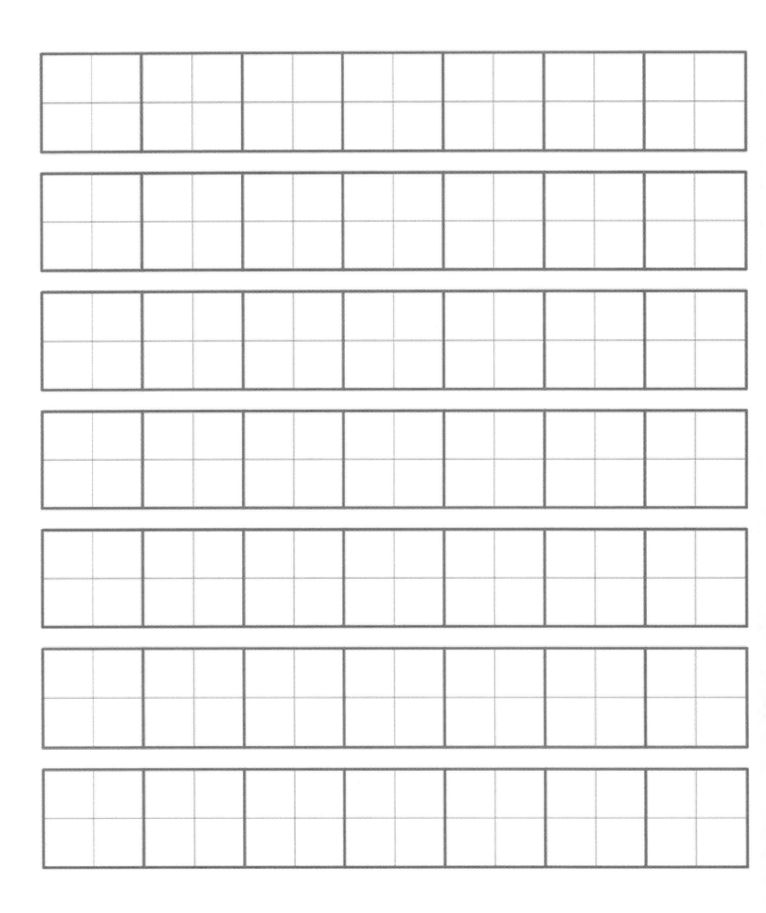

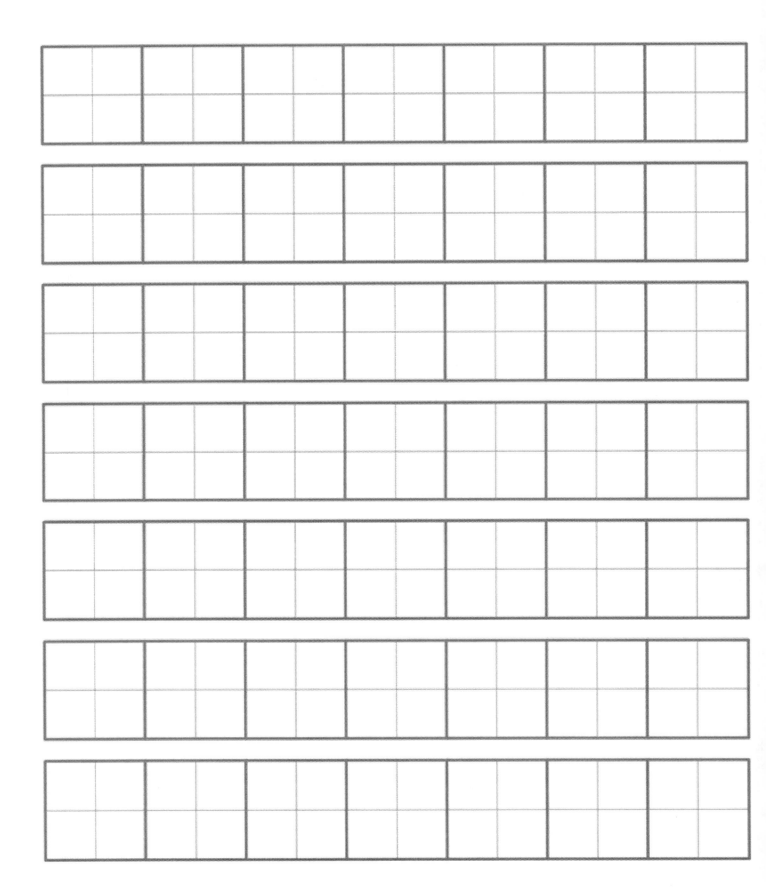

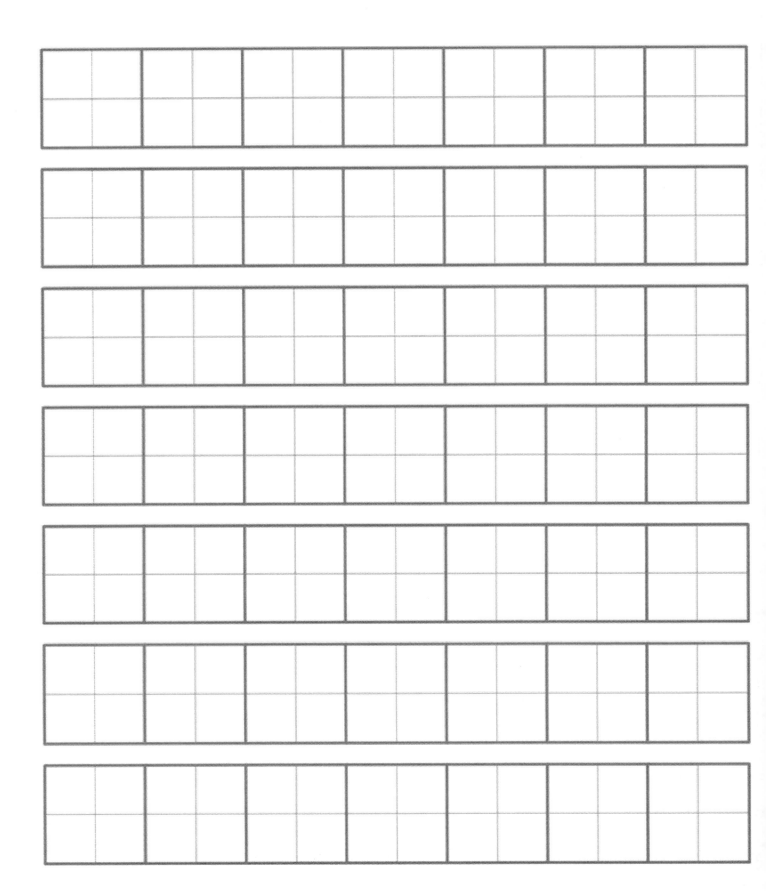

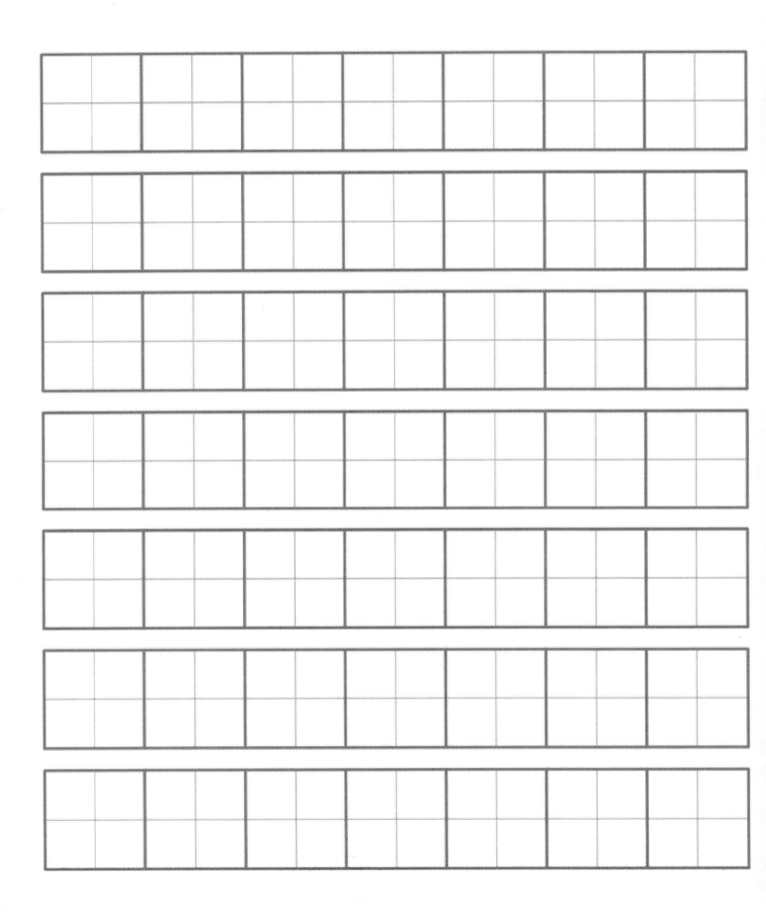

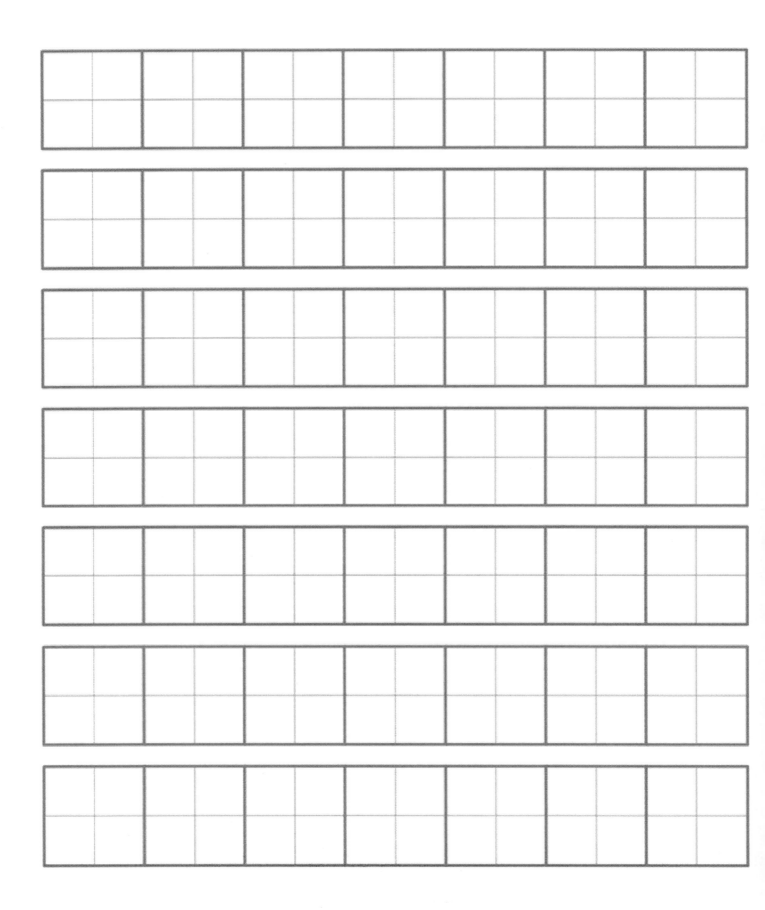

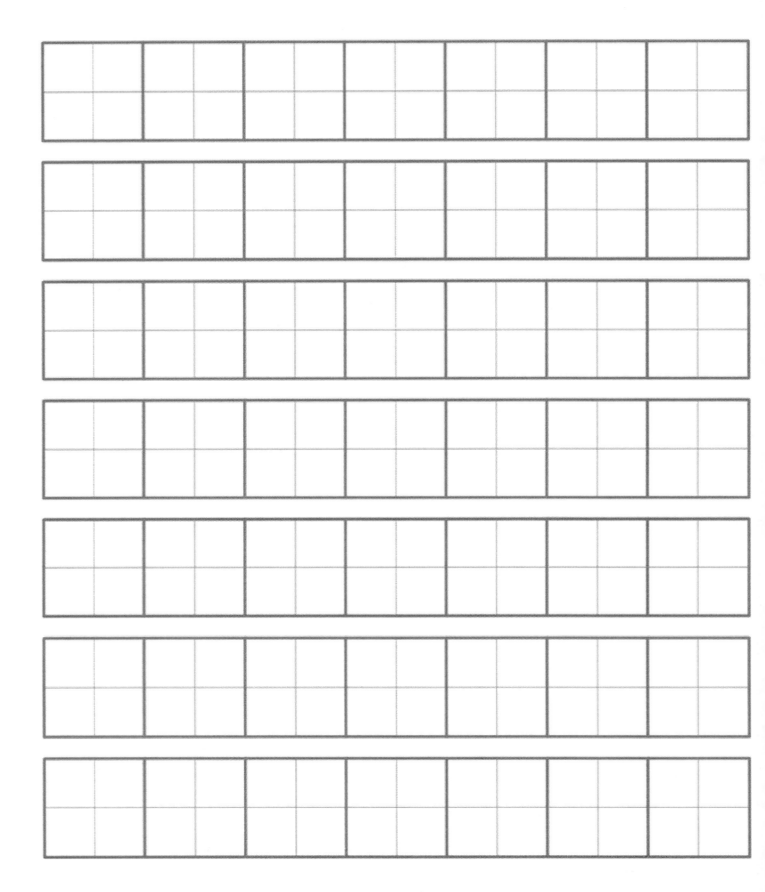

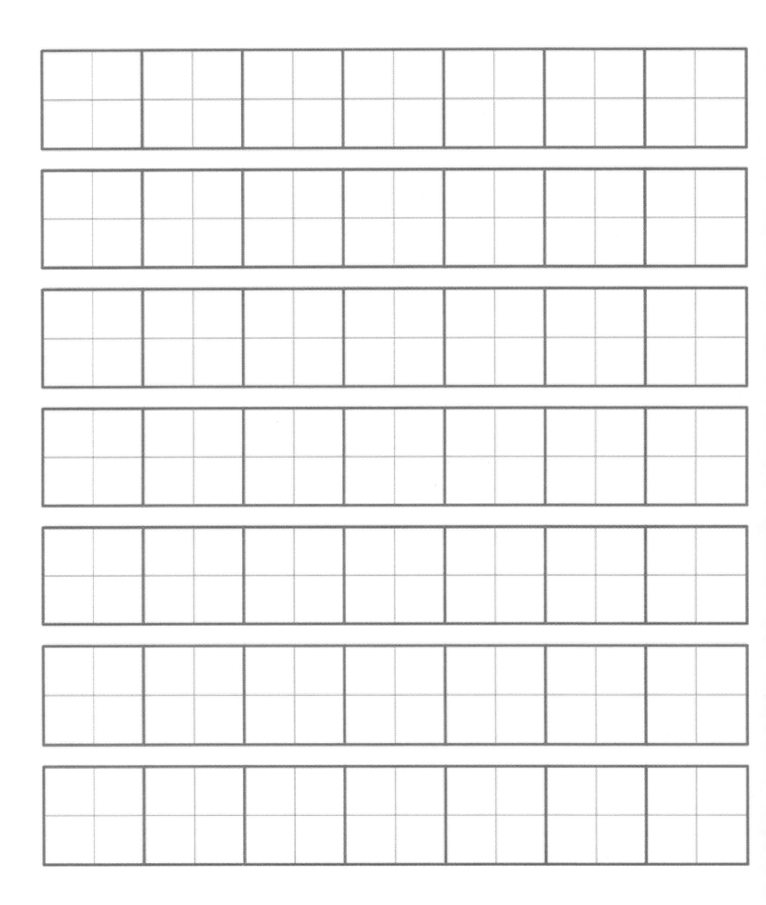

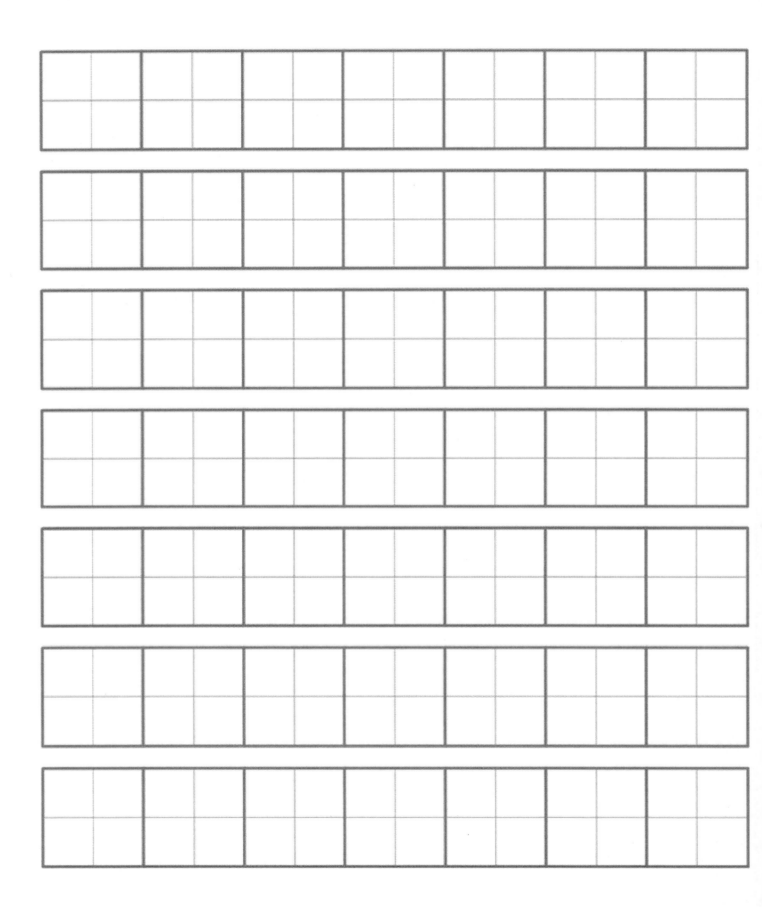

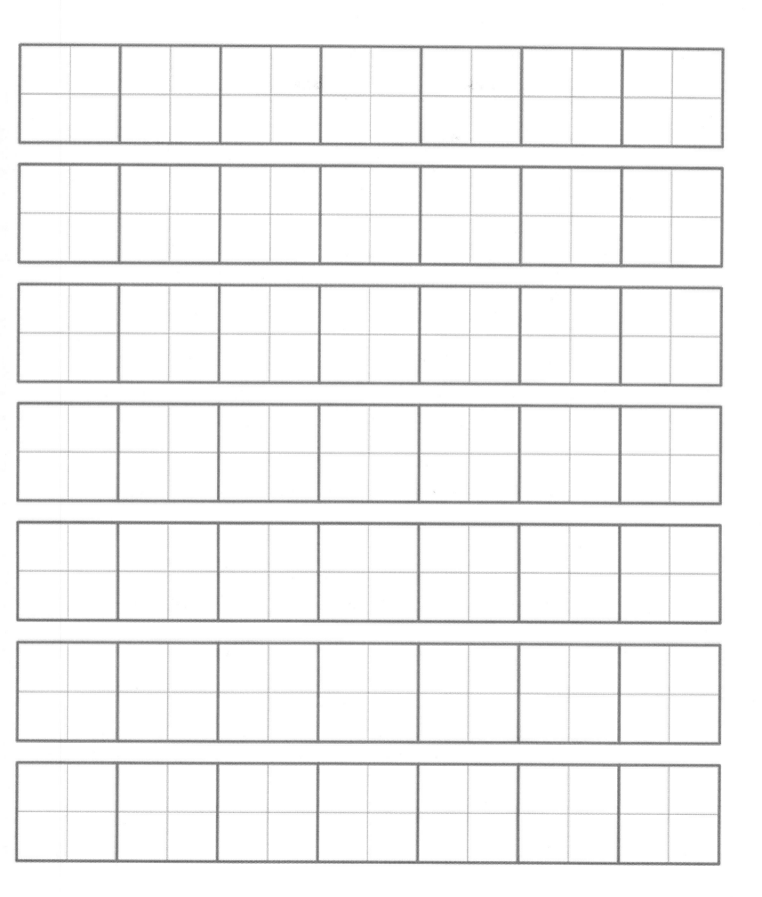

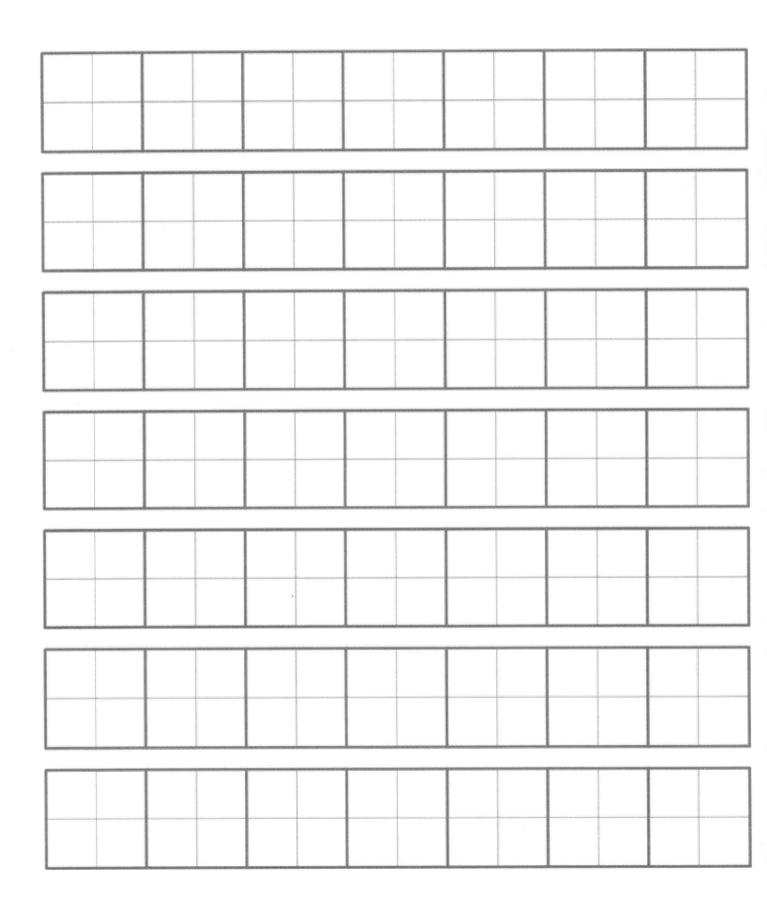

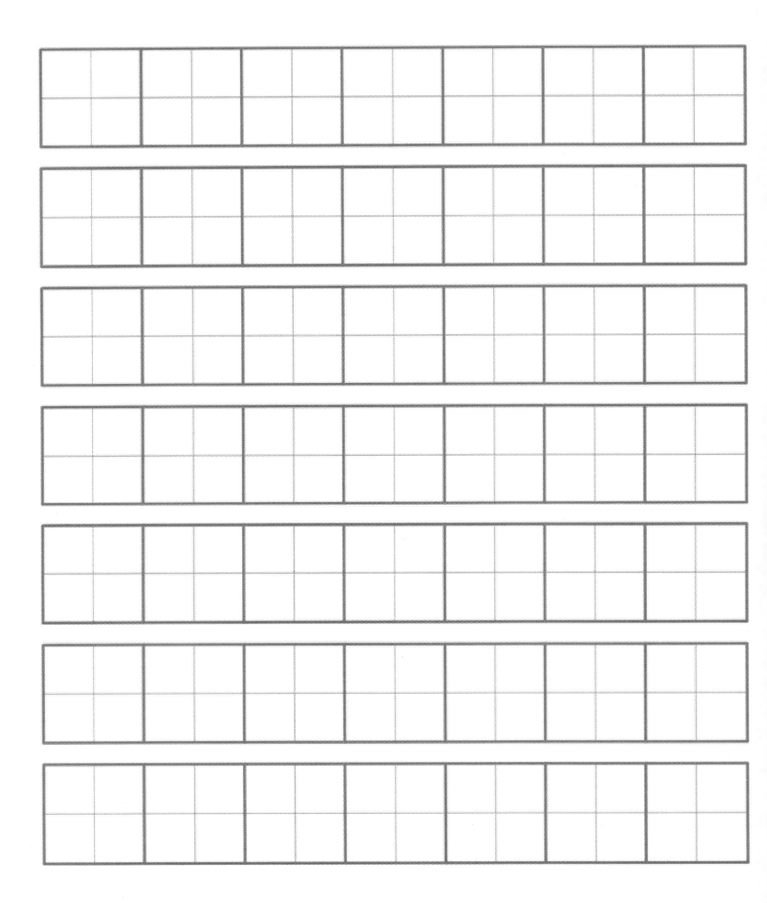

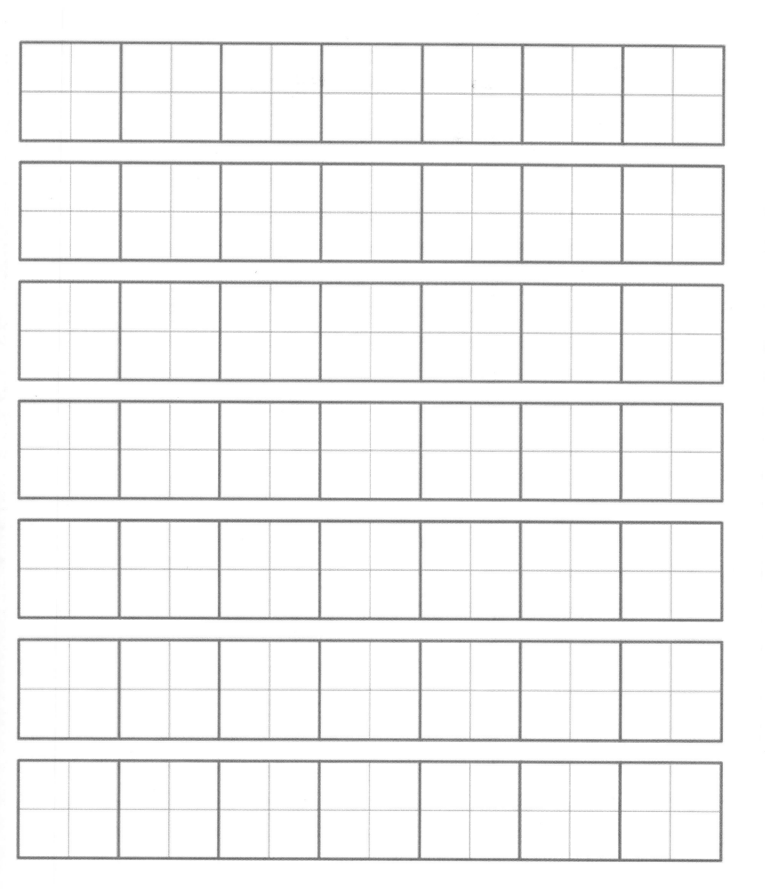

Made in the USA
Las Vegas, NV
29 March 2022

46490237R00059